River Spells

poems by

Meredith Heller

Finishing Line Press
Georgetown, Kentucky

River Spells

*To the Yuba River
My temple, my lover, my muse*

There is another alphabet, whispering from every leaf,
singing from every river, shimmering from every sky.
—Dejan Stojanovic, from *Forgotten Home*

Copyright © 2021 by Meredith Heller
ISBN 978-1-64662-625-0 First Edition
All rights reserved under International and Pan-American Copyright Conventions. No part of this book may be reproduced in any manner whatsoever without written permission from the publisher, except in the case of brief quotations embodied in critical articles and reviews.

ACKNOWLEDGMENTS

Thanks to the amazing editors at Rebelle Society for first publishing many of the poems in this collection, often in different versions.

Publisher: Leah Huete de Maines
Editor: Christen Kincaid
Cover Art: Lucy Pierce—www.lucypierce.com
Author Photo: Meredith Heller
Cover Design: Elizabeth Maines McCleavy

Order online: www.finishinglinepress.com
also available on amazon.com

Author inquiries and mail orders:
Finishing Line Press
PO Box 1626
Georgetown, Kentucky 40324
USA

Table of Contents

Part One

Page 1

Part Two

Page 14

Part Three

Page 23

Part Four

Page 27

I'd see her
Soaking
In the water
Soaking
Up the sun
Singing
Like a mermaid
On a rock
For everyone
Some nights
I'd camp
Beside her
Staring
up at stars
And poem for poem
We'd swap
Our rhymes
And strum
On our guitars
Sometimes
I'd come to find her
But she'd have slipped away
Up where
the river's wilder
Immersed
in verse
For days

–Obo Martin, singer/songwriter & storyteller

Foreword

River Spells is a collection of short poems I wrote in the summer of 2019 while camping at the Yuba River in Northern California. I was healing from a bicycle crash that shattered my right wrist requiring three surgeries and six months of relying solely on my non-dominant left-hand. Yes, to neuroplasticity; it was a time of restructuring everything I knew about myself. Like the way I love to write with pen and paper. There is something about the feel of my pen pushing against the texture of paper that opens the doorway for me to translate the poetry I feel in my body, into words. But there I was trying to type poems on my phone with my left thumb, and just when I thought I would go crazy, I had a flash to write short nugget-poems – like spells, that conjure the essence of a moment, heighten consciousness, and leave one transformed. A spell is understood as a short period of time, as in – get away for a spell or a rainy spell. It's a brief shift into the liminal, like a dizzy spell or a fainting spell. It is a duration of time spent deeply engaged in an activity, such as a spell of garden work. We spell out words and we can spell it out slowly for someone. According to Merriam-Webster, in *Spelling Out the History of 'Spell,'* in Middle English, the word spell meant *to mean* or *to signify*, and from the Germanic, spell comes from *gospel* which translates as *good tale*. The article exclaims, *Language is magic!* And of course, a spell is a form of words used as a magical charm or incantation to bring about change; how very poem-like.

Stay wild!
Meredith Heller

Part One

1
It's happening!

The sky is swimming
pink and blue fish
chase each other
across the river's surface
catch each
other's reflection
before they dive under
dragonflies
tilting the horizon
rocks taking off
their stone masks
unfolding their limbs
stretching their gray bodies
into the water
and watching me
with their creature eyes

2
Sometime
just about now
the river's face flushes
the mouths of the rocks
part their lips
to speak
what they've known all day
and the jade water
grows darker
moving downstream
like it's got somewhere
it needs to go
and all night
the insects sibilate
the stars shimmy

      How could I ever be lonely?

With all this life
thrumming through me

3
There is a moment
when the birds
decide it's morning
when the sun blares
his brass horn
when everything
green and growing
starts crawling
toward the light

The sun puts his hand
on your shoulder
and the great cacophony
of the river
opens its mouth
and sings

4
In the morning
you must greet the day
sweep the sand
fill your water bottle
from the spring
step into the jade river
as it gurgles
the morning news
from rock to rock

Whisper your prayers
to the water
wave to the cloud people
who are shapeshifting
into dragon riders

Devote
yourself
to the day

5
If you put your arm
across your eyes

at high-noon
you can catch
the sunflowers
blooming in the dark

6
There's a boy named River
who comes around here
sleeps in the trees

Makes love
to a bottle of vodka
he traded for his teeth

Pans for gold in the morning
shows me his treasure
in the palm of his hand

I read him a poem
and his eyes
fill with tears

*There is more
than one kind
of treasure*

7
My first swim
to the far side
of the cove
where river nymphs
drape lithe bodies
over sun-baked rocks
their tribal tattoos
wake and slither
into the water
dragonflies dance
in druid circles
gathering morning's
harvest

8
When the river rocks are wet
their colors come to life
you can spend hours hunting

agate
    serpentine
        bloodstone

But let them dry
and your treasures
turn dull as dirt

mouse brown
    charcoal gray

Put the people
in the river
watch them
shine up
like jewels

9
R I V E R

    The sound
        of the word itself
            implies current

10
If I were getting married..

I wouldn't get married
    at the river

I would get married
    in the river

11
    —*For Laura & Janice Gates*

I believe in magic

The way
we weave
in & out
of each other's worlds
when we most need it

The way light
draws more light
a living helix
braiding itself
stronger

This morning
as I walked
to the spring
to get water
I ran into an old friend
and her sister
on the trail
asking for directions
I welcomed them
down to my camp
at the river's edge

All morning
we held council
while the water
worked her magic
her fluid fingers
her circles of song
undulating our joints
singing our cells
back to life

Three water witches
each of us shining
a mirror
in which we see
ourselves more
clearly

Janet, river sprite

swims merrily
sheds her years
rides the rapids
until she glows

Laura, illuminator
intuits my shattered wrist
as an opportunity
to stop working
from my body
and share my voice

I offer the path of *the hum*
the heart-compass
the clear bell that rings
when you move
in the direction
of what you love

Follow
   what makes
      you hum

We were hitting
the crescendo
when the osprey
came winging
just above our heads
so close
we felt the breeze
of his feathers

He played
two high notes
on his golden coronet
and day was done

12
Around the next bend
a blackberry bush
pink flowers
and ripe berries

hot from the sun
feast until your fingers
and mouth are purpled
with desire

Climb up
to the rock perch
in the shade
watch the water
spill in torrents
of bubbling lace
absorb the heat
from the rocks
into your body
until you melt open
and the sound
of the current
sweeps your blood
clean

And then
      the blue heron

13
Today the river
is clear as glass
I can see
all the way
to the bottom
rocks and fish and light
creating underwater labyrinths
where the water
wends her way
through the dark

14
All day
I wait
for dusk
to wrap

her pastel cape
around
my coppered
shoulders

Whatever it is
you're tying
in a knot
in your belly
your breath
will free you

15
Paint your body tribal
with crushed river rock

Lie naked
in the water
until you
become
the hum

16
Waning light
smooths the wrinkles
of the river's face

17
Milk the day for joy
fill an extra jar
for a thirsty friend

18
Sleep outside naked
all night the stars
kiss your body
and bloom
in your blood

19
*Did I mention
I married the river?*

We consummated
our union
last evening

    The sky blushed

The river slid
a gold ring
on my finger

and we roared
with joy

20
So many beautiful people
come to the river
singing songs of gratitude
in languages they learned
from Native Americans
Eastern Indians
Peruvian Shamans

I wonder if the spring
and the cedar trees
yearn to hear
original songs
melody & words
that bubble up
in the moment
from our own
heartspring

So this morning
as I drink
from the spring
and breathe
the scent of cedar
I listen for a song
in my heart
and I sing

Thank you Spring
   thank you
      for everything

Thank you Cedar
   without you
      I could not be here

I open my voice
embroidering a melody
along morning's golden seam
feeling I've truly given
something of myself
in gratitude for all
I have been given

And in the singing
my heart is doubly-full

I walk back to camp
adding to my song

the Sky
    the Sun
        the Rocks
           the River

And they all sing back to me

21
Get up early enough
to catch the clouds
bellowing lavender smoke
from their underbellies

Wash your face
in the river
dive deep
let her swallow
you whole

Float downstream
singing songs
of thanks

Swim back
against the current
until your heart pounds

I'm alive
I'm alive

22
Sit on the edge
of the big rock
see your shadow
in the water

Remember our time here is brief
before we all become shadows

> *What kind of watermark*
> *will you leave?*

23
The dragonfly circus flies in
every morning at 10am
practicing their aerial acrobatics
swinging on silks of sunlight

Enchanted, I muse,
bring the knife thrower
and the pretty lady in sequins
who dances
on the back of the horse
bring the strong man
and the fortune teller;
heck, bring the freaks!

We're all beautiful
in the water's mirror

24
I heard the man
who invented drones
modeled them
after dragonflies

The way they

HOVER

in place

Highest & fastest
flying insect
ancient friends
of dinosaurs

I got one tattooed
across my upper back
when I was 30
art nouveau wings
straddle my shoulder blades
a caduceus
twists medicine
down my spine
through the tail

My river ally

25
Murmuration
   of sunlight
      on water

26
    —*For Victoria*

Climb down
chimney rock
get close to the river
plunge your head

into the current
rip in ululation

Beat out songs
of thanks
and forgiveness
on the rocks
with sticks

While Victoria
plays the charango

Forgive all
your past lovers
who left scars

Thank them
for how strong
and true
you've become

Leave wet footprints
      across granite stones

Part Two

Song of the Sun

As soon
as you hear
the song
of the sun
in the morning
get up!

Add your voice
to the chorus

Morning

Morning
sends her birds
with their silver flutes
her fish jumping
to catch the sun
in their scales
her water
braiding the light
a cairn
of heartshaped rocks
balancing
on a boulder

Halleluya

*Halleluya
it's morning!*

Everyday
I grow
younger

Emerald Pools

Walk past
the white fence
up the hill
around two ravines
where the river
changes course
and everything
goes fey

Turn left
down the first fork
then right
through the bridal trees
and the forest
of young cedar
to the Emerald Pools

Dive into cool
green velvet
swim upstream
to hidden beach
climb into stone ovens

Listen to the *riverspeak*
feast on wild blackberries
sing thank you
in a hundred
new melodies

By Order of the Queen

The River Queen commands:

> *Off with Their Clothes!*

Blue Eyes Shining

The holiest

of life's children
come by here
sometimes

Skin and bones
wrapped in rags
walks into the river
with his boots on

Greets the day
smoking tobacco
from an apple pipe

One crazy arm
dancing to music
only he can hear

Pulls a few words
from a pocket
of lost language

> *Light will gather*
> *Light must disperse*

I choose
to befriend
even the most
neglected
parts of myself

Says goodbye
with a toothless smile
a hand on his heart

Blue eyes shining

Fish

Lie still
in the water
long enough

the fish
come find you

Flecks of gold glinting
through transparent flesh
as they nibble your toes

We become
what we
imbibe

Wake

I hear
a lot of people
at the river
identifying
as woke

In my experience
it's not something
that happens once
and you then
get to spend
your days
floating
peacefully
downstream

It's a thing
we must
wake new
in ourselves
each & every day

Sun Goddess

Sun Goddess
wakes me
this morning

her light singing an aria

I was tracking
dream creatures
in the dark

*Can we do this later? I ask,
I'm not done sleeping yet*

She explodes
in a chorus
of spiral galaxies

singing
    spinning
        laughing
          yellow
      orange
   gold

And the wind
        licks my cheek

Rest

Today you can simply rest
breath will fill and empty
from your lungs
water will flow downstream
wind will stroke the water
sun will paint the rocks

Later

Later
you'll swing
down the trail
where there's no one
but the river

You'll make love
in the sunlight
on the rocks
with her soul

Teach Me

Teach me, river
to keep flowing
no matter what

Teach me
to seek empty space
rather than fighting
against obstacles

Teach me
to keep singing
even when
I doubt myself

Teach me
to welcome everything
as an essential part
of the web of life

Teach me
to cut through
resistance
with patience

Teach me
to position myself
where the light
can touch me

Where even
my shadow
becomes beautiful

Lakota Man
            —For Victoria

She listened
to her heartbeat
followed it
to the drumbeat
of Sundance
in South Dakota
where she offered
cedar & tobacco
made her prayers
at the center
of the universe
where four dragonflies
hold the four gates
of the four directions
Met her Lakota man
in the sweat lodge
connected
by the umbilical cord
of their birth year
they touched
a river
between them
learning
each other's
songs

Float

F L O A T

The Bargain

I was lounging
like a mermaid
on the rock

half submerged
legs dangling
in the water

back melting
into hot granite
when the water snake

slid over
in her satin
one-piece

stopped
two inches
from my hip

I yelped!

She held
her head high
and said,

I remember youuuu
we met right here
last summerrrrr

I've grown big
and brave,
she said

I see that, I said
still a little
wary

Well, she said
I just came overrr
to say heyyyy

She tasted the air
with a flick
of her tongue

*I won't bite you
if you put me
in one of your poemssss*

Full Moon

Full moon
paints her face
in the water's
reflection

River Dirt

River dirt
Good dirt

The kind that
lays claim
when you play
outside all day

Fingernails caked in mud
hair tangled tinsel
skin laced
with mineral white

> *Dirt in my smile lines*

Part Three

Lie Still

Today simply
lie still
on the big rock
listen to the rapids roar
feel the cool air
feather your body
as the clouds gather
as the wind lifts
your sarong
as the green eyes
of the river
watch you

Acceptance

Morning wakes me
with hot hands

I guess I forgot
to post my
DO NOT DISTURB
sign at my campsite
because all night
two sweet smoking boys
laughed and whooped
it up until dawn

I teetered
back and forth
across the edge
of sleep
catching shooting stars
in the corners
of my eyes

The woodswoman
arrived at first light
chattering about

the people-puzzle
in her home
shares her breakfast
of calf's liver & nettles

I rise reluctantly
pull an angel card
from her bag of tricks

I get ACCEPTANCE

> *The only path
>   that ends suffering*

All morning I practice
while the naked yoga people
do planks & headstands
on my morning rock

An elderly man
in a fishing hat
blares NPR
from his phone
and tells me,
*We have to learn
to share*

I suggest,
*I could
share
a pair
of earbuds
with him*

I lie in wait
on a flat stone
bathed in light
nibbling an energy bar
until the yogis
bow off
with their Namaste
and I reclaim
my morning throne

A tiny dried flower
greets me
pink petals
against
gray stone

Beautiful Mess

I'm sitting
in the river
on a rock
carved
by Picasso

Thinking back
on my life

> *Huh, what a mess!*

Well, the river responds,
A beautiful mess

Floating

Floating
at night
on my back
in the river

no distinction

between
body
water
night sky

held together
by some
invisible
force

stars
sizzling
my
bodywatersky

Confluence

The river says
joy and sorrow
come from
the same place

They are two currents
of the same river

Follow the flow
of either one
and you grow
your capacity
for the other

One is easy
downstream
you simply let go

The other
more challenging
upstream
you gotta work

They are both easy
and they are both hard

You Choose

Eventually
they become
a confluence

Part Four

1
In the morning
bubbling merrily
with wide arms
and bright face,
she wakes the world
stroking each rock
each grain of sand
my heart rises
emboldened

2
I try to count
how many different
shades of green
roll down
the river's back
but I get distracted
by the way the light
bends through the water
prisiming in infinite
mosaic

3
There is
simply
nothing
like
swimming
in the river

Then emerging
and fitting
your curves
against curves
of hot granite

Where
you meet
a secret

shared
between
bodies

4
Ms. Snake
  made us all
    laugh today
      she came up
        sunning
          on a tip
            of rock
              sticking out
              of the water
          her tail
        lashing
      back & forth
    in the current
    obviously
    enjoying
    herself
   part of
   the party
     on a Tuesday
      afternoon
        at the river
          she said,
          You're
          luckyyyy
          I invited
          youuuu

5
Have you ever
seen anything
as blue & infinite
as this sky?

6
In the dusk
we hunt
for jade

Sitting in the river
telling jokes
sifting rocks
through our fingers

All stones
are unique
but some
are more
unique
than others

7
Let this be
the last summer
I sleep under
a skyful of stars
thrilled
with the great
mystery
alone

8
You can't sleep
under all these stars
and believe
we are the only planet
in the entire cosmos
with life

9
I woke this morning knowing
that there is nothing
that is not part of everything
there is only everything
alive
breathing
being
together
in interdependence
and we are
part of it

10
All night
the river boys
smoked & plucked stars
from the strings
of their sitar

I rocked naked
in the hammock
under the trees
letting the last
dregs of sorrow
evaporate
from my bones

11
Smoke faeries
come on the dusk
play Celtic tunes
from lonely town
drop their bodies
in the river
like stones
surrender
their skin
to the sky

12
The lesson of the river:

    Let it go ~

Meredith Heller is a poet, singer/songwriter, educator, and author of *Write a Poem, Save Your Life* and three poetry collections. A California Poet in the Schools, she leads workshops for grades 1-12 in public and private schools, Juvenile Detention Centers, Women's Prisons, and online for women and teens. She is avid nature-woman who spends her summers camping beside rivers and oceans. She lives with a gentle footprint in a tinyhome in Northern California.

For info about her workshops: www.meredithheller.com

www.ingramcontent.com/pod-product-compliance
Lightning Source LLC
LaVergne TN
LVHW041603070426
835507LV00011B/1279